Basic principles of marriage

8 keys for a successful and healthy marriage

By

Brandon M. Dotson

Introduction

At first, when all we have is each other, we pay close attention to the fundamental components of a strong and happy marriage. But as our marriage progresses, "stuff" starts to collect and takes our attention away from the fundamentals of what makes a happy marriage.

Suddenly, the assessment value of our house causes us more concern than the worth of our marriage. We often examine the status of our retirement accounts before our marriage. Or we neglect the person in our bed in favor of caring for the automobile in the garage.

Our houses and lives start to fill up with things, and soon they start to demand our money, time, and valuable energy. As a consequence, we don't have much left over to take care of the essentials of a good marriage.

Wise couples understand that although having a good house, vehicle, or retirement account may seem lovely to have, these things alone may not guarantee a happy marriage. They realize that there are far more crucial factors at work.

They have discovered the importance of spending money, time, and effort on the following eight factors for a happy marriage:

Copyright

Table of contents

Chapter 1

Love/Commitment

Being dedicated to another person is the essence of love.
In contrast to what is shown on television, the big screen, and in romance novels, it is much more than a transitory sensation.
Feelings come and go, but a sincere commitment to one person lasts a lifetime, and that is what makes a marriage healthy.

Through the good and the bad, the ups and the downs, marriage is a commitment.
Commitment comes naturally when things are going well.

But genuine love shows itself by sticking together through difficulties.

There are several reasons why love is essential in marriage.
Marriage is, after all, not always a simple arrangement.
You could never have the motivation, focus, selflessness, and patience necessary to make your marriage a long-lasting success without love.
Let's examine the role that love plays in marriage and how it helps people and marital wellness.

What does marriage love entail?

Since love often serves as the glue holding a marriage together, love and marriage should ideally go hand in hand.

It could strengthen your relationship with your significant other.
Marriage love is not static; it develops throughout time.
You go from the honeymoon and puppy stages of love to a love that develops over time.

The kind of love you feel is shaped by a variety of live events.
Your love will be more robust the happy your marriage is.
But if there are unresolved toxic issues in your marriage, the love will also be poisonous.

Additionally, passionate love alone is often insufficient as a foundation for marriage.

For it to be fully effective, it often also has to have romantic love, friendship, and compatibility.

Because of your aggravation with the situation, your health and relationship may suffer in a marriage without love.
It could cause you to lash out in ways that harm your marriage, such as cheating or acting out of anger.

How does love appear?

Depending on your stage of life and what it contributes to it, love may take many various forms.
You may be wondering why love is so significant.
What makes it unique?

Love might seem like radiant sunlight that casts a rosy glow over every aspect of your existence.
You may get a constructive viewpoint as a result, which will improve how you handle situations.
However, love may also seem to be a bad thing if your marriage has several unsolved problems.
These may complicate your situation and put a shadow over all you do.

Eight advantages of love in marriage

A happy marriage may significantly improve your life.
Your perspective on things, your moods, and even your health may be affected.
See how love may enrich your marital and personal life by looking at the

different advantages of love stated below;

1. Increases contentment

Love encourages joy.
Whatever you may think about being independent and free, nothing compares to the security and comfort that comes from knowing that someone is watching out for you.
Dopamine is a neurotransmitter that is produced in the brain's "Reward Center" when you are in love.
Therefore, it should come as no surprise that dopamine stimulates pleasant feelings and makes you feel valued, pleased, and rewarded.
Love also causes the level of the stress hormone cortisol to rise.

While cortisol is sometimes thought of as a "Stress Hormone," in the case of falling in love, it doesn't make you feel nervous but instead causes the butterflies in your stomach, excitement, and intense passion you experience during the first stages of a new relationship.

Even when you transition from puppy love to adult love, some research indicates that your dopamine levels could stay high.

2. Boosts the immunological system

Your immune system might be strengthened by having regular intercourse with a caring spouse.

Compared to single people, married couples had reduced incidences of

depression, drug misuse, and blood pressure.
Additionally, people who live alone are more likely to get heart disease than those who are married.

3. Strengthens monetary security

When it comes to your money account, two is better than one!
Compared to unmarried or divorced people, married couples are more likely to enjoy financial stability and build up more money over time.

Couples who are financially stable have less stress, less debt, and more flexibility in their marriages, especially if one spouse can only work part-time or prefers to remain at home to take care of kids or other duties.

4. Fosters respect

What aspect of marriage is most crucial?
respect and love.

Any wholesome connection is built on respect.
Love and trust cannot develop in the absence of respect.
When you feel appreciated, you are aware that your words, ideas, and emotions are important.
When respect is shown, you may readily trust.

Emotional support is a crucial aspect of respect and love in marriages.
You are more able to be open and confide in your relationship when they

respect your thoughts and treat you properly.
Emotional support has a good impact on one's entire marriage, mental health, and level of happiness.

5. Higher-quality sleep Is there any factor that makes love in marriage important?
You will sleep better when you are cuddling with the love of your life, blanket hoggers, and score hounds aside.

According to studies, couples who slept together had lower cortisol levels, more restful sleep, and faster sleep onset than those who slept alone.
Love is crucial in a marriage for this reason.

6. Lessens tension

Your mental well-being may also benefit from the value of love in marriage.

According to studies, loneliness may harm your health and even make your brain's pain centers more active.

Anxiety levels rise when a person is alone.

Love and sex are very effective in preventing stress and anxiety.

Oxytocin, a calming hormone, is released in part to accomplish this.

This "love drug" is in charge of the connection you experience when you touch the person you love, whether it's via an affectionate act like holding hands or an intimate one like having sex.

Additionally, oxytocin reduces stress and balances your neurochemicals, which makes worry and tension go.

7. Lengthens your lifespan

One University of Missouri researcher found that couples age more gracefully than singles do.
According to the Department of Human Development and Family Studies, married people generally assess their health as being better than single people, regardless of age.

Another advantage of a happy marriage?
In addition to having a statistical advantage over unhappy singles in terms of lifespan, this research found

that being single was the most important indicator of early death.

It is believed that the emotional, social, and economical support acquired from being a member of a "couple" has an impact on a married couple's long lives.
As an example, married partners are more likely to have access to healthcare.

Males who are married live longer than men who are divorced or who have never been married, according to Harvard research.
This is assumed to be a result of married males cutting down on some aspects of their lifestyle after getting

married, such as drinking, arguing, and taking unwarranted risks.

8. strengthens your relationship

In a marriage, having a fulfilling sexual relationship is essential since it physiologically binds you to your spouse and makes you feel amazing to be near to them.
Oxytocin is a hormone that promotes bonding and is often referred to as the "love drug." It is produced when you touch your lover.
It inherently improves sentiments of love, confidence, trust, and optimism.

There is no limit to the significance of love in marriage.
It improves relationships, improves sex, and lessens the stress and anxiety

of everyday life. It also has health advantages.
Without love, it would be impossible for you and your spouse to have a happy, fulfilling relationship.

last thoughts
The presence of love in a marriage has several advantages.
It may increase your sense of security on all fronts—emotionally, cognitively, physically, socially, and financially.

A loveless union leaves much to be desired, but when two people are married, they have more strength to deal with issues and overcome challenges as a team.

Although it is not a very "sexy" term or idea, commitment arguably has more

to do with keeping marriages together than anything other than shared beliefs.
It involves more than simply exchanging wedding vows and obtaining a marriage license.
Because our behavior changes when we are aware that our futures are intertwined, commitment is crucial.
If you are aware that the other person won't be around forever, you may decide to avoid a difficult talk.
If your present love has a crippling injury or begins to irritate you, you could find another one.
A commitment is a vow to stick with something and see it through, not only today but always.

A commitment is a decision to renounce options.

This gives a lot of flexibility and complexity, even though it first may seem restrictive.

The dedicated person is no longer forced to decide which person or manner of living would make them happier.

When one commits, all of their efforts are focused on seeing it through.

Other options are no longer a diversion.

Making the first commitment and sustaining the commitment are the two key phases of commitment.

1. Taking the first step and committing

Making the first commitment has been a major focus of study on how commitment affects marital satisfaction.

Social scientists often compare couples who live together before getting married to those who do not.
Cohabiting couples are assumed not to have yet made a solid and irrevocable commitment to be together "until death do us part" or else they would be married.
The future of their marriage depends entirely on this tentative or partial commitment.

According to Dr. Scott Stanley, a marriage researcher, people who cohabit before becoming engaged do worse after getting married on almost every metric than those who wait until marriage or wait until after engagement.
This comprises:

psychological hostility
Interaction that is bad (conflict)
They feel confident in their connection.
marital contentment
commitment to one another

This danger may be partially explained by the ambiguity and lack of mutual commitment present when cohabitation first starts.
The nature of cohabitation presupposes the likelihood that a marriage may not last (and thus the commitment not being permanent).
If they subsequently get married, it may not be so much a "deciding to marry" as a "falling into marriage."
The clarity of the commitment gets muddled when the choice to be

married becomes less clear and more of a slow slope into marriage.

No of one's money, color, or culture, slipping will be more dangerous than choosing.

Because of the mutual clarity and ensuing follow-through, deciding will always be linked to lesser risk.

Additionally, the data demonstrates that women are more adversely affected when they transition from cohabitation to marriage.

In these relationships, the women are more devoted to their husbands than the husbands are to their wives.

2. Honoring the agreement

While the phrase "until death do us part" might seem dreadful, it can also sound quite lovely.
Most couples still think they are committing themselves permanently when they get married, regardless of whether it is in a religious or secular ceremony.
We all know that the divorce rate ranges from 40 to 50 percent, but most couples who get married don't anticipate getting divorced.

What transpires between the formal exchange of marriage vows and the choice to file for divorce?
There is no "one size fits all" solution in this case.
Undoubtedly, some couples chose to be married when they were too young, too eager, or too gullible.

Others either had additional character faults that were disregarded or were not readily apparent during courting or were not mentally developed enough to "forsake all others."
Others just became bored or worn out from attempting to make it work.
Others diligently toiled and gave their best to the union, yet their spouse ultimately decided to divorce them.
An absent spouse cannot be wedded to someone.

For their safety or because their partner won't work on the marriage, some spouses have no alternative but to elope.
However, studies demonstrate that many marriages might be saved if the commitment is strong (Waite and Gallagher, 2000).

After five years, three-fifths of the formerly unhappy couples who had been married reported being extremely happy or pretty happy, according to Waite and Gallagher's assessment of a large national sample of unhappily married couples.
Along with significant amounts of time, therapy, work, luck, and faith, a couple may sometimes get through tough times just because of their dedication to one another.

The slogan of the Marriage Encounter movement is: "Love is a choice."
It serves as a reminder to couples that despite how amazing love is, it is not enough to sustain a marriage.
Husband and wife must resolve to love even when they don't feel like it at

some point (or rather, many moments).
Love is rekindled when you decide to pay attention to your marriage and follow through by doing kind things for your spouse, speaking softly and politely, and making this choice again.

Making a commitment that lasts a lifetime is important to couples who recognize that it involves much more than merely deciding not to get a divorce.
It's a commitment to carry out the everyday tasks necessary to maintain the commitment.
To hear each other's worries, it could be necessary to switch off the television or go for a daily stroll.

The building blocks of commitment include activities like these and several more.

They are the behaviors that maintain a marriage dynamic, engaging, and intriguing to fend off temptations to make a different decision.

Although persons of all faiths may get married, Christians may want to consider the verse that says "take up your cross every day and follow me." (Luke 9:23)

We reaffirm our commitment to follow our loved ones each day, and vice versa.

Chapter 2

Sexual Faithfulness

Sexual fidelity entails being loyal and true to the marital bed.

This is often explained in terms of abstaining from affairs, watching porn, and other vices.

These are fine things to stay away from, yet they are just one aspect of loyalty.

The development of good traits is also necessary if one is to be loyal to God and practice Love in the marital bed.

How do your sexual behaviors amplify God's love?

If they are not, you are not fully adhering to God's intentions for sexual activity in marriage.

For instance, it is not true to the Divine intention of love freely offered when having sex is only duty or task.
The Divine sexual vision of intimate understanding, creative goodness, and sensuous beauty are not faithful when sex is just used as a way to release unfulfilled sexual energy.

It's a plus if you've never had sex with someone else while being married.
Sexual fidelity, however, entails more than just "not having an affair."
To be completely true to one another, you must respect each other's sexual preferences for your union.
When we don't truly develop our sexuality to its full potential, we deprive our partner.

Sexual unhappiness may be a sign of this immaturity.
And the "one thing" that's still missing may be bringing a genuine passion to your sexual life.
This involves far more than just not "acting out" and calls for a change in your inner views.

Why does temptation remain when you are in a relationship?
It's like putting a couple's notion of loyalty to the test.
Nowadays, we observe an increasing number of married couples ending their marriages due to troubles, and one of the most prevalent challenges in this situation is fidelity.

No one intends to cheat on their wives, so when it happens, it comes as a

surprise. However, can you truly call it an accident?
Is meeting someone else truly destiny or merely the result of making bad decisions and breaking your vows?
Do you realize there are several methods to define fidelity as well as techniques for enhancing it?

What does loyalty entail?

What does it mean to be loyal to your spouse? We may know the term and have perhaps used it often.
Did you realize that this phrase has so much more to it than just being used to describe a spouse or romantic partner who won't commit adultery?

Three sincere explanations for marriage

The notion of loyalty in marriage extends beyond abstaining from adultery.
In truth, there are three categories in which we may classify the true meaning of loyalty.

1. A definition of faithfulness (Duties as a Spouse)

A committed spouse will faithfully carry out all of their responsibilities toward their partner.
One of the promises we would make when we were married to this person was that we would take good care of them and try our best to uphold our obligations as their spouse.

This goes beyond merely supporting our family monetarily.

It entails appreciating that person above everything else, along with love and living life together.

Marriage is much more than simply physically being there and taking care of things like the bills, the mortgage, and the food.

One of our responsibilities as partners is to appreciate your spouse as a person and value their opinions, views, and emotions.

One approach to demonstrate your loyalty to your spouse is in this manner.

2. Definition of faithfulness (Being Trustworthy)

While our vows were sincerely spoken, the ultimate test of your word loyalty will come as the months and years go by.
Everyone should be prepared to be dependable with the smallest promises and the greatest fidelity tests.

Say white lies to people?
Are you a trustworthy spouse who can maintain your words and your commitments?
Can you perform faithfully without others noticing, including in your thoughts and feelings?
Most individuals mistakenly believe that only adultery-related behaviors may sabotage faithfulness, although lying, so-called innocuous flirting, and deceptions are all behaviors that can undermine one's confidence in loyalty.

3. a definition of faithfulness (Being Loyal to your Spouse)

When it comes to marriage, this is the definition of fidelity that is most often used.

You, as a married person, shall never longer attempt to get into another marriage and will withstand any temptation that you may meet in addition to being faithful to your vows.

We must be oath- and heart-bound loyal when we are married.

We shouldn't contemplate any behaviors or statements that may entice us into flirting or that could put us in a position where we could commit adultery or sin.

While some could argue that temptation is just part of our nature, there are other arguments in favor of the idea that we always have control over our actions, regardless of the circumstances.

Depending on what we decide, we will either be true to our spouse or unfaithful to someone else.

ways to increase fidelity

A decision to be unfaithful is never made by mistake.

So, even while we have the option to give in to temptation, we also have the option to resist doing so and focus on ways to make our commitment to our spouse stronger.

Here are some suggestions on how you and your spouse might make your marriage stronger through fidelity.

1. Comprehend one another

You will know your role in your marriage if you and your partner can communicate well.

Your marriage won't always be blissful and ideal.

Trials and misunderstandings are inevitable.

You are more likely to be unfaithful if you are weak and just consider getting even or that you don't deserve what is occurring.

Instead of concentrating on how you might mend your marriage, you will see the "what ifs" of life and turn your attention elsewhere.

Being unfaithful begins with that.

2. Honor one another

Can you lie to your spouse if you love and respect them?
Can you withstand the suffering you'll cause your spouse if you cheat on them or begin speaking lies?
No matter how little your defense may appear, a lie is a lie, and it spreads.
Even during difficult times, respect keeps your marriage together.

3. Be accountable for your life.
What do you do if you see that your marriage isn't working out?
Do you find solace in another person?
Play the victim card?
Or maybe simply search for someone to meet your needs rather than focusing on the need to save your marriage.

This won't work; eventually, you'll realize how damaging these behaviors may be to your marriage.

You must understand that marriage requires two individuals to work together to achieve success.

Don't expect your marriage to succeed if you lack the fortitude to accept responsibility.

The meaning of faithfulness in marriage varies depending on the individual.

We might define faithfulness in our marriages differently, and we might also be going through trials and tests to see how faithful we are.

There will be temptations, and the majority of them provide an "easy way out" of marital issues or may serve as some people's "go-to" remedies.

There are many possible explanations and justifications for why someone cannot be faithful, but they are all still choices.

Do your best to be loyal, keep in mind your promises, and keep your aspirations in mind.

Chapter 3

Humility

Staying humble when in a relationship might be difficult.
A marriage, however, requires an equal amount of giving and taking.
Do you want to learn how to be more modest?
Do you often question yourself, "Is humility a good thing?"

Or do you wonder how to be modest in a relationship?
You may strengthen your relationship with your spouse by learning how to be a more humble partner from this article.

To better serve your spouse and yourself, it may educate you on how to humble yourself in marriage.
Or do you wonder how to be modest in a relationship?
You may strengthen your relationship with your spouse by learning how to be a more humble partner from this article.
It may help you better support your spouse and yourself by teaching you how to humble yourself in marriage.

Acts of humility might be helpful when you're trying to figure out how to be more modest.
Being humble enables you to keep the delicate balance necessary for the Marriage to operate and to provide a loving, encouraging atmosphere.

Everyone has diverse thoughts, views, and perspectives, which might sometimes conflict with those of our relationships.
Gaining self-awareness may help you better comprehend your spouse and build a strong, harmonious connection.
Lack of humility may lead to confusion, and misunderstandings, and has even been implicated in relationship breakups.
There are several benefits to being modest and displaying humility in your marriage.

Can power come from modesty?

Acts of humility may appear obvious when discussing how to be humble in your relationship.

Unfortunately, when we work together as a team, these little gestures of humility are often overlooked.
This often occurs as we become used to our routines.
Being humble demonstrates to your spouse your concern and regard for them.
Even though it may seem simple, there are a few methods to be humble in your relationship.

To cultivate humility, you must:
Pay attention to what people are saying.
Ask questions to help you understand and explain
Keep your eyes on the prize.
Recognize your flaws and shortcomings
Acknowledge your mistakes.

Recognize that you are not aware of the thoughts and feelings of others. prioritizing others above yourself Adopt a sympathetic stance Study people and their cultures.

View things from a viewpoint other than your own Have the self-assurance to admit when you don't know something and be open to learning Offer an apology without being asked and beg for pardon when appropriate Be thankful for every opportunity you are given in life.

Ten ideas to improve your relationship's level of modesty

You may be modest in a variety of ways.

While some come easily, others need effort on our part to achieve.
We offer 10 straightforward ideas that might be useful if you're wondering how to humble yourself in a relationship.

1. Recognize the value of others' opinions.
Although receiving unsolicited advice might be annoying, it can also be beneficial.
It's common for others to see things that you are blind to.
Other people's viewpoints may sometimes provide you with new information that you had not thought about.
Being humble entails searching inside oneself for things one may alter.

Always have an open mind when someone provides advice and make an effort to understand it from their perspective.

The height of humility is realizing that there are times when other people know more about your life or your deeds than you do.
It is essential to learn how to humble oneself in a relationship.

2. Develop your hearing
Many of us neglect to practice our listening skills and often take them for granted.
It might be challenging to concentrate on what is being said and comprehend the content in a society where multitasking is encouraged.

The ability to effectively communicate depends on it.
Showing your spouse that you are paying close attention demonstrates your interest in and respect for their viewpoint.
You may improve your understanding of one another and become closer as a pair by listening to your mate.

3. Take criticism graciously.
It might be difficult to see the advantages of criticism when it occurs.
However, criticism enlightens us by pointing out our flaws and assisting us in correcting them.
It is through criticism that we improve as humans.
When you get criticism, don't get irritated; instead, think about the value it offers.

Pay attention to the criticism and consider the veracity of the assertion.

Humility requires us to accept our shortcomings, even if they might be difficult.
Through acceptance, cultivate humility and utilize it to inspire personal transformation.

4. Recognize your weaknesses and faults.
We must learn to accept criticism as well as to own up to our mistakes.
You are not an exception; nobody is flawless.
Understanding that you are flawed like everyone else is a sign of humility.
You must own your shortcomings and seek to fix them if you want to be humble in your relationship.

While being open to new experiences is essential for personal achievement. Failure is equally important.
Without mistakes or flaws, life would be meaningless.
Recognize your weaknesses, capitalize on them, and build a better future for yourself.

5. Express your gratitude without bragging about what you have.
Being grateful for all of your benefits is wonderful, but boasting is not.
You may have graduated at the top of your class or received honors and scholarships for your volunteer work with the underprivileged, but none of this counts if you did it simply to enhance your perception of yourself in the eyes of others.

People with modest personalities are aware that the greater picture matters more than just themselves.
Do nice deeds purely out of virtue and not to bolster your college application.
Sincere actions of humility are those that come naturally and are intended to enhance everyone's life, not just your own.

6. Accept discomfort and promote change.
The pain that humility may cause is among its most difficult characteristics.
Discomfort, despite how it feels, is a positive thing.
Although we may not first welcome the change, it is paving the way for a better, brighter future. This is what humility's pain reminds us of.

7. Regularly express your gratitude

Even though it may seem obvious, one of the worst regrets in life is often not expressing gratitude.

People's wellness, as well as your own, may be greatly impacted by showing people that you value their work or actively expressing your thanks for their part in your life.

The phrase "thank you" is often used, and for good reason—it has a great impact.

According to recent research conducted by the University of North Carolina at Chapel Hill, showing appreciation has an impact on both the individual expressing it and anybody who observes it.

As a result, using these straightforward phrases will help you strengthen relationships and trust.
Keep an open heart and mind, and never stop being grateful for the people in your life.

8. Concentrate
Being attentive to and interested in your partner's life is one of the simplest ways to be more humble in your marriage.
Learning to be more watchful is a useful skill.
You may develop humility by being aware of how you treat other people, and you'll discover more about yourself in the process.
You will be able to see the broad picture and address any problems you may be having by practicing humility if

you are alert and paying attention to the environment around you.

9. Recognize your talents and shortcomings.

It is not necessary to feel sorry for yourself or minimize your achievements to learn humility.

Understanding your talents and flaws and constantly putting both in perspective are key components of humility.

Humility is the ability to resist the impulse to seek approval from others and to seek such approval from the inside.

Being modest and possessing humility entails developing the ability to comprehend other people's perspectives and seeing the world from a different angle.

10. Give thanks for everything.

It's not about making loud, overt demonstrations of devotion that knock on doors and demand attention when you want to be modest in your marriage and life.

It is a simple, often invisible deed in daily life.

Cooking supper, doing a task without being asked, or purchasing your partner's preferred snacks when grocery shopping are all examples of humility.

Putting another person before yourself is an act of humility since their pleasure is equally as important as your own.

You may find the solution in your reflection if you're wondering how to humble yourself in your relationship.

Conclusion

A successful existence includes being modest, which is essential for a happy marriage.

While you can question if being modest is a good thing, it's important to keep in mind that humility is more about what it can do for others than what it can do for you.

The ability to be modest in your personality and your marriage may tell you a lot about your spouse.

Better still, it can teach you something about who you are.

It is worth the effort to learn humility since it is a necessary ability.

Therefore, keep in mind to go inside yourself for the answer while

questioning how to humble yourself in a relationship.
Although it begins with you, being humble influences everyone you come into contact with and has the power to create or destroy a relationship.

Chapter 4

Patience/Forgiveness

According to our experience, for a marriage to succeed, patience is a need.

So much so that we think it's one of the crucial marital skills that each couple should master and put into daily practice.

Because you can't successfully communicate with each other without patience.

How will you be able to discuss money, have sex, and settle disputes without getting into a fight?

We will thus discuss what patience in marriage entails in this post, along with six doable strategies for improving your patience with your spouse.

What is meant by patience?

Tolerating things or controlling your want to lash out in rage or frustration is what we mean by having patience.

Let's examine this common example:

Have you ever had a sluggish computer or one that takes forever to start up?
When the computer was sluggish, what did you do?
Either you waited quietly or you started grumbling about how sluggish the computer was.
(Or repeatedly press the button, as my wife does!)

Did the computer work any quicker for you in either scenario?
No is the obvious response.
However, you were either patiently waiting or whining, which had two distinct effects on you.
You were calm and cheerful while you waited for the computer to load.
However, when you complain, it's like you're up against a wall and it annoys you (your patience for waiting is gone), so you get upset.

We can all understand that having patience will make us happier based only on this example.

What does marriage patience mean?

This entails having patience with your partner, your children, and your marriage.
Being able to restrain oneself from uttering cruel words to your partner during an acrimonious exchange is another definition of patience.
In other words, refrain from berating your partner.

Additionally, it implies we must be patient with our spouses when they inadvertently cause us pain or annoyance.
When our relationships aren't what we want them to be and when our kids constantly press all of our buttons, we have to have patience.

Imagine insulting your partner or kid because you were upset about something little they did.
When you know you can't take those comments back, how do you feel?
Not a good sensation, is it not?

This sensation alone suggests that the best course of action when we are irritated by our wives, kids, or other people or things is to be patient.

6 realistic techniques to increase your spouse's patience

1. Always work on being patient.
The skills you need to be patient with your spouse are acquired when you practice being so with your friends, family, children, coworkers, etc.

Additionally, if you have children, being a patient parent will provide your kids with numerous opportunities to learn how to be patient as well.
They are closely observing you.

2. Constrained technology.
Keeping technology and other distractions to a minimum will help you be more patient while also improving the quality of your discussions.

When I use my phone, I've observed that I get angrier when my spouse and kids attempt to speak to me.
When people attempt to speak with me, I have made it a point to put my phone down.

I'm not perfect, but every day I work to improve.

This has made it easier for me to be more in the moment, which has improved our relationship and my capacity to be more understanding when they need to talk to me or ask me a question.

Find out what triggers you.

This requires patience and deliberate work.
So, work on being patient every day, particularly with the tiny things that could otherwise irritate you.

Additionally, attempt to pinpoint the situations and people who might quickly make you impatient.

For instance, words that incite rage and/or defensiveness in you, feeling stressed or hungry, being ill, the way you communicate, etc.

Look more closely at what makes these things irritate you.

Additionally, take note of your mistakes when you lose your patience.

Next time, try to be more patient!

Keep in mind that patience is essential for a successful, joyful, and rewarding marriage.

4. Be mindful of the time of your talks.

Be cautious while attempting to start discussions that could be more complex.

Wait until you are both at ease and have some alone time without interruptions before engaging in a deeper or maybe more emotional talk.

Saying, "Honey, I want to speak to you about __, so let me know when you are ready," can help you prepare your spouse for the discussion (as we previously indicated).

Longer discussions aren't the only time when it's advantageous to give each other a heads-up.

By letting your partner know that you need to talk to them, you offer them the chance to stop what they are doing or complete it so they can give you their whole attention.

In our daily lives, from asking each other questions to remembering to do things around the home, and everything in between, we have found this strategy to be extremely helpful.

Alternately, if your partner approaches you with a chat and you sense your irritability building, halt.

"I know you want to speak about this because it's important to you, but I'm just not in the appropriate frame of mind to give you the attention you need on this subject.
Can we postpone this discussion till ?"

5. Control your anticipations.
This implies that you must acknowledge or express your expectations for your partner, the discussion, or the result of your communication.
Effective communication is mostly dependent on managing your expectations.

You may need to sometimes reduce your standards and accept modest steps.
Having realistic expectations might make it easier for you to be more patient with your partner since you will both be aware of the bigger picture.
It enables you to see the larger picture rather than being mired in the current circumstance and its associated feelings.
The virtue of patience!

6. Enjoy a rest.
Take a pause when you feel your patience waning.
Sometimes all it takes is a little pause of five minutes to let you relax and respond more effectively than react.

How patience may strengthen your marriage.

Generally, being patient will help your marriage in the following situations:
When having a respectful argument with your spouse.
It enables you to deliberate before responding or speaking.
When you are conversing with your partner and they are not listening to you or paying attention.
If your children are disobedient, making a mess, or refusing to complete their duties.
When you and your partner are having trouble speaking about matters like money, sex, chores, etc.
Your conversations will be more courteous and relaxed, which will improve your ability to communicate.

If your marriage isn't what you'd want it to be.
Being patient will let you be a listening ear when your spouse begins to express their frustration after a trying day.
And when your partner can do that, it demonstrates their willingness to be vulnerable with you.
a simple action you may do if your spouse is impatient.
If your partner lacks patience, you may encourage them by setting a good example.

For instance:
I'll confess that in the first year of our marriage, Marcus had more patience than I did.
His patience eventually paid off for me.

Since then, I've learned and developed patience.
I realized that I would be very upset if he snapped at me as harshly or rapidly as I did at him.

So why would I do this to him again?
After a heartfelt apology, I started the difficult process of teaching my wife patience.

last thoughts
According to our experience, having patience is a valuable ability to have in your marital toolkit since it is so essential to a happy marriage.

More significantly, a lack of patience in a marriage may be disastrous and quickly result in regrettable words or deeds.

We strongly advise you to make every effort to be more patient with yourself, your partner, and your marriage.

So put into practice the simple concepts you just learned to be more patient in your marriage and with your spouse.

Chapter 5

Time

Making time for your marriage: 8 steps
I frequently wonder where the day's hours went at the end of the day and then reflect on how I could have utilized those hours more effectively. Lost time can never be found again, as Benjamin Franklin once said.

Possibly, you can relate.

Making time to truly invest in your marriage is difficult enough when trying to get everything done in a day. However, research indicates there are valid reasons to make time specifically for your spouse.

Researchers found that the longest-married couples cited their shared memories—memories that take some time—as a key factor in the health of their relationships in a study published by the Australian government's Institute of Family Studies.

Expert opinion

We spoke with experts this month to bring you eight doable suggestions for spending time with your spouse and putting your marriage back in the spotlight.

1. Make time by going more slowly.
You must first make time for your spouse to give them time.

Consider the activities that consume your time and consider how you can make more time for your relationship. "Eventually, love on the run will turn into love on the rocks.

Simplifying your life and purposefully concentrating on the things that matter to you are necessary for slowing down.
This is intimate behavior on purpose."

2. Make time to converse with each other, and not just listen!
Couples are advised to communicate directly and continuously for no less than 30 minutes each day, as this "inoculates your Marriagefrom stagnation and degeneration."
She claims that this conversation will enable you to go beyond just sharing

information and into a deeper type of interaction, which she claims is the foundation for true intimacy.

3. Remain aware of each other's specific requirements.
According to Shannon Battle, clinical director of Family Services of America, ignoring a partner's needs may cause a couple to drift apart.
She claims that everyone wants a partner who is a skilled mind reader.
"However, if wants are not expressed, nobody can inform you about them.
Even if you spend the whole day together, you will still be total strangers."

4. Experiment with new things; it will benefit your health!

Make a date out of it if you're purposefully making time for your relationship!
According to Doares, novel encounters encourage the release of good neurotransmitters in the brain.
Want some inspiration for your art?
See our selection of fantastic date ideas.

5. Avoid letting "homework" consume too much of your time.
In their 16 years of marriage, military spouse Cari Andreani has managed to balance her job commitments with her husband's six-month deployments.
In these kinds of circumstances, you have to be resourceful with your time, Andreani advises.
"I will arrive at work early, take care of things during my lunch break, and

even stay a little bit after work to finish my job so that I may spend time with my spouse.

I leave everything at work so that when I go home, I can concentrate on my family."

6. Get close to one another, despite the difficulty of the situation.

Couples may sometimes feel emotionally unprepared for certain life chapters and feel overwhelmed.

"According to her, it becomes intolerable, lonely, and painful, and individuals begin to believe they have lost love.

Under a layer of frustration, anger, feeling misunderstood, and powerlessness on how to improve the relationship, the love has been buried."

According to Dr. Harrell, it's crucial to support one another and keep your affection for one another in mind through trying times.
Remember that you love each other and that the current situation is difficult.

7. Continue to put your marriage first.
Your marriage may start to suffer when other responsibilities need your focus; often, this may happen without your knowledge.
Ask yourself every day whether you are purposefully spending time with your partner.
"I don't know anything, even marriage, that lives on neglect,"

8. Invite God into your day-to-day activities.

Roland Hinds, a marriage guru and the author of Are You Right For Me? Whose Decision Is It Anyway? emphasizes how crucial it is to have God at the center of your marriage.

He advises creating useful routines, such as daily group prayer.

He claims that "where the closeness starts and should [be] maintained in a couple's relationship is by allowing God a place in that connection."

Chapter 6

Honesty and Trust

If you or your spouse often questions whether they are hearing the truth or a lie, then your marriage is over.

The layers of deceit, "white lies," and "casual falsehoods" corrode a marriage's core basis.

When trust is lost, it might take a long time to regain it as well as the need for complete honesty in a marriage.

Your level of affection for one another will grow as you establish honesty in your marriage.

Because you will have a deeper knowledge of each other's hearts via honesty, your oneness will grow.

Three areas where couples may actively take action to develop or preserve honesty in the everyday fabric of their relationship have been identified by our research on marriages.

These aren't structures created because a person doesn't trust their partner.

Instead, out of a desire for togetherness and oneness at any cost, they become normalized.

When fostering honesty in marriage, focus on the following three areas:

1.

HONESTY IN FINANCE

It is unnervingly typical for married couples to conceal money and transactions.

This article states that "Nearly 7% of the more than 1,000 respondents questioned on behalf of CreditCards.com confess to keeping a hidden bank account from their spouse or partner.

ANY concealing of money dealings is dishonest and destroys confidence in a marriage, according to two-thirds of respondents, who also admitted to having a secret credit card account and forty-five percent, a secret savings account.

Even if it goes unnoticed, the needed deceit introduces attitudes and behaviors into the marriage that quickly erode harmony.

Have an open-door policy as a relationship.

Both of you have easy access to pay stubs.

You and your partner may both examine your bank statements and internet accounts.

You everyone are familiar with your own internet accounts' passwords.

Practice making all of your transactions transparent, including the coffee you purchased on the way to work!

Be careful to first reach an agreement and then discuss (and pray!) any significant purchases.

Spouses have been known to buy trips, automobiles, vehicles, and other things without first consulting their partner.

God has given you the resources you share so that you may manage your assets and money as a team.

2.
Honesty in emotions

"Honey, how are you doing?
"Fine." (Even if they aren't!)
Or "Are you upset?
" "NO!
(When they are, of course!)
or "What are you contemplating?
When they seem to be considering or obsessing over something, say, "Nothing."

Because you have a better knowledge of how your spouse is thinking about and responding to life's circumstances,

emotional openness helps to create trust in a marriage.
According to Dr. Willard Harley, "Your desire and capacity to accept one other's sentiments are what makes a marriage effective.
An otherwise happy couple may experience extreme sadness when life's circumstances change if they are not given the truth underlying those sentiments.

Decide to choose to express your feelings honestly.
To achieve this, you must commit to acting in a kind, considerate manner that respects Jesus' presence in your life and marriage.
Your hearts will become entwined in an ever-deepening love as you share

more about what is happening inside of you both.

3.
MEDIA ACCURACY

Our buddy who is a counselor once informed us that he counsels 90% of the affairs that began on Facebook.
Someone looks for a former high school love interest, a former coworker, or a close buddy from long ago.
or communicating privately with a new acquaintance who piques your interest.

Secret email accounts may be used to deceive the media.

The login information for the other spouse's phone or computer may be concealed from one spouse.
Because porn has been seen, history files are wiped from computers, phones, and tablets.

You may take the following actions:

Have complete access to and disclosure of the passwords to every electronic device the two of you possess.

Install online accountability programs like Covenant Eyes or X3watch.
Make sure your spouse has your passwords and give them full access to your social media accounts at any time.

You can't prepare for every scenario, but starting and upholding media honesty in your marriage goes a long way in preserving the honor of your union and trust.

By improving your honesty in these three areas, you will be strengthening your marriage.

The Importance Of Honesty In Marriage

Most people would agree that lying is never a good idea, particularly in a relationship.

So what subject is the most likely to persuade married couples to lie?

Money.

According to a recent AARP research, 33% of married persons between the ages of 18 and 49 have kept purchases

from their partner a secret, and 7% even have a secret bank account!
Fascinatingly, older poll participants were far less inclined to tell their partners a lie about their finances.

So why do so many ordinarily truthful individuals lie when they have access to joint finances?
And not only that but lie to the one with whom they ought to be the most honest?
Whatever the reason, the reality is that it's a bad habit that might cause your relationship to lose trust.
Think about Why Honesty is Non-Negotiable in Marriage and commit to being honest, even when it's difficult.

Each of us has assets and liabilities.

However, one flaw in a marriage that you must tolerate is a propensity for deceit or dishonesty.
Being dishonest will cause even the smallest problems in your marriage.
This is why:

It's a precarious slope.
You will feel quite uncomfortable—the first time—if you lie about anything that seems innocent (like whether you followed your diet today at lunch).
It will be simpler the next time you do it.
You'll progress to telling falsehoods shortly concerning matters of more importance and discover, hopefully to your shock, that you've become very adept at it.
Then there's the whole mess of having to lie to cover your tracks on a

previous transgression: you spent $300 on a pair of must-have boots, but told your husband they were marked "way down." Now you have to figure out how to justify why you don't have enough money to pay the auto insurance premium, even though you should.
It just isn't worth it.

It undermines faith.
Regardless of how minor the issue was, once your spouse discovers that you have been dishonest with him, he will find it more difficult to believe you when you say what you mean.
It will be more challenging for him to trust you with the things he values, even if he forgives the dishonesty.

Until that trust is rebuilt, it could seem like a cloud of unease and tension is hovering over your marriage.

It provides a poor example.
Your kids are far more perceptive than you know about the subtler aspects of your marriage than you may assume.
On the phone, they will overhear you giving your best buddy one account of the events while giving your husband another one.
Even if they never come out and expose you, your credibility with them will be severely harmed.

Your family's objectives are harmed by it.
Don't be shocked if your family doesn't end up where you had envisioned it if you and your partner have mutually

agreed upon a set of objectives and a strategy for accomplishing them but you insist on going your way in secret.
Your family's prospects of achieving crucial financial objectives, such as paying off debt or saving for education, are jeopardized if you covertly violate your agreed-upon financial plan.
Don't be shocked if your child experiences negative consequences if you covertly allow them to flout the rules that you and your husband established as a parenting team.
A house divided, as they say, is not a happy house.

The simple line is that living together may be challenging.
In a constantly changing world, we have challenging children to raise,

debts to pay, occupations we don't always like, and unforeseen surprises along the road, some good and some awful.

If you can rely on one another, you can get through it all.

Be open and reliable with your spouse to give your marriage the best chance of success.

Being completely genuine, straightforward, and transparent in our words and deeds is what it means to be honest.

It entails adhering to a few fundamental principles, like never telling lies, never concealing the truth, and never purposely leaving out or distorting the truth.

Being completely open and truthful with your spouse about both major and little issues is what it means to be honest in a marriage.

You aren't being honest if you avoid discussing issues with your spouses, such as those that are upsetting you in the union, actions you took that you know would make them angry, or your true feelings on topics you discuss.

Being sincere means never disguising who you are, what you believe, or how you feel from your spouse.

Since trust in a relationship depends on honesty, trust is essential for a marriage to survive and prosper.

Being consistently honest with someone lets them know they can rely on you and what you say.

Knowing they can trust your pledges and promises is beneficial.

Marriage and well-being coach Shula Melamed, M.A., MPH, explains to me that since relationships are based on trust, being honest with one another is crucial.

We rely on our spouse to be a confidant with whom we can share our ideas, emotions, and hearts.

Being open and honest with your spouse encourages wholesome communication, which is essential for a functioning relationship.

True connection requires that partners be able to communicate honestly and freely with one another.

Since both parties are committed to being open and honest, any tension, arguments, or other problems in the relationship will be addressed on the

front end by being brought up to their partner for discussion.
Marriage counselor Margaret Paul, Ph.D., has said to be that "relationships prosper when partners trust each other to be honest and open to resolving a disagreement."
On the other side, when trust is betrayed, partnerships fail.

In a marriage, honesty is very vital at all times.
Each lie that your spouse exposes you to weakens your relationship and transforms you into adversaries in an unspoken struggle where your word is never taken seriously, says Melamed.
"Having said that, there is no need to be ruthless when giving your opinion or responding honestly to queries that you know can be hurtful."

For instance, if your spouse just prepared the worst dinner you've ever had and inquires about it, you should be honest and not claim to enjoy it when you don't.

But Melamed advises staying away from remarks that are excessively unpleasant (such as "you're a poor chef") and opting instead for nicer methods to express the same idea.
I am so grateful that you prepared dinner tonight.
But do you find it a little bit bitter?
Or, "I find it to taste a touch bitter, therefore I believe there's potential for improvement.
However, it's obvious that you put a lot of work into it, and I value it when you prepare supper.

Privacy vs secrecy

Couples may sometimes get too preoccupied with attempting to learn every last detail about one another.

For instance, a person could insist on sharing an email address or always be aware of their spouse's whereabouts, or they might feel free to compliment their partner on their choice of celebrity even if it offends them.

According to marital therapist Linda Carroll, LMFT, "clearly, there are occasions when revealing too much might potentially be undermining your independence and feeling of self—or worse, injuring your spouse."

Understanding the distinction between secrets and privacy is crucial.
Think of privacy as a wall surrounding one's thoughts, ideas, and experiences from the past that do not specifically include one's spouse.
A secret is anything that is purposely kept concealed from others out of concern for criticism or retaliation.

Though they don't have to share every detail to be deemed honest, partners must be open and honest when discussing matters that might negatively impact one another's well-being.

As a general guideline, if you're purposefully delaying informing your spouse about anything because you're concerned about their response, you're being willfully dishonest.

Additionally, you must be honest if your partner directly asks you a question.
Being honest doesn't require you to divulge every detail to one another.
However, it's critical to be open and honest when discussing details that will directly impact one another's well-being.

How to improve a relationship's level of honesty and trust

1.
Be reliable.
Be a reliable partner by carrying out the things you claim you'll do.

Melamed believes that establishing trust requires more than just words: "Show up when you say you will.
Make good on your promises.
Empty or unfulfilled promises are the best way to undermine trust and foster animosity.

2.
Avoid making commitments you can't keep.
Since they don't want to let anybody down, many feel obligated to pretend they can make it and show up for someone else even if they can't, according to Melamed.
"It's better to be upfront now and cause a little bit of disappointment than to be upfront later and damage trust."

3.
Put communication first.
Establish open communication as a top priority in your relationship.
Talk to each other and make a deal, to be honest about how you're feeling, what you need, what's working, and what isn't.
By setting this example, you make it simpler for both of you to practice being honest.

4.
Set an example.
Is your spouse distant or inconsistent in sharing their emotions?
It takes time, not pressure, to get someone who is closed off to open up.
Simply setting an example for them is a terrific approach to encourage

children to feel comfortable being sincere.

Inform them of your thoughts or plans while giving them the freedom to follow you.
Your spouse will feel comfortable being honest with you if they see that you are constantly being honest with them.

5.
Don't evaluate one another based on what they say.
People are less likely to want to be honest in the future if they express how they feel to their spouses and are subsequently silenced or screamed at for what they say.

Therefore, it is best to refrain from passing judgment on or condemning someone who is being open and vulnerable.
That entails refraining from labeling what they stated as "dumb" or informing them right away why their feelings are incorrect.
Honesty is bred when individuals feel comfortable expressing themselves, therefore you want to foster that environment.

If someone says something that offends you, thank them for being honest, and then talk to them about why it made you feel that way.
Did they have another method to tell you that would have hurt less?
Notify them.

You may let someone know that knowledge is something you would prefer not to hear from them if they mentioned something you truly wish they hadn't.
Just keep in mind that part of being in a relationship is having someone who can tell you unpleasant things.

6.
Address the violations
Both couples must devote serious therapy attention to their marriage when trust has been destroyed in a partnership, according to Paul.
To comprehend why the betrayal led to shattered trust, each individual must examine themselves and work to mend their portion of the relationship system.

Trust that has been damaged requires time and diligent, serious effort.
You two must work together to figure out how to regain that trust.
Paul continues, "Don't fool yourself into believing that you can restore damaged trust with a hasty declaration of forgiveness and a warm hug.
To ensure that betrayal doesn't occur again, the root causes must be found, investigated, and dealt with.

7.
Time it out
Trust grows over time.
It's hard to just push oneself to trust someone when you're not quite there.
Find strategies to help you feel comfortable and protected in your relationship.

It will be crucial to start by pledging to be completely honest with one another over and over again.

The lesson

Although it can occasionally be challenging, being honest with your partner is the cornerstone of a strong relationship.
These seven suggestions can increase honesty and trust in a relationship if you or someone you know has trouble being truthful.

Belief in each other

A marriage in trouble is one where there is no trust.
It is hard for a marriage to succeed if there is a lack of trust in it.

An essential component of creating and maintaining a happy marriage is trust.
One of the most vital aspects of your relationship, and an essential component of any lifelong commitment, is your ability to trust one another.
Your marriage's quality will suffer without trust.

Why does trust matter to you?

Trust is essential to healthy relationships and also has a significant impact on your level of happiness.
You may feel safe, protected, and supported if you can trust your spouse.
Marriage is a lifelong commitment, so it's crucial to know the person you're

tying the knot with is someone you can confide in your fears, ideas, and emotions in.

Why does your spouse value trust?

For the same reasons that trust is vital to you, your partner needs to feel secure, content and supported in your relationship.

As the Sacrament of Marriage is about forging a lifetime bond, you and your spouse must have mutual trust to support one another through every stage of the relationship.

when there is no trust

It is quite challenging to have a loss of trust or a breakdown of trust in a relationship.

It also negatively affects a marriage as a whole.
After a trust violation, partners may become angry, wary, and vigilant of one another.
If both of you are willing to work together to rebuild trust between you, it is possible to do so and repair breaches of trust.

However, if a lack of trust persists for a long period, it may do irreparable harm to a marriage or relationship.
It may be challenging for someone to trust their spouse if they had previously been the victim of a trust violation in their family of origin or during a prior marriage.
It's critical to discuss your past experiences with your spouse in these situations so they can better

understand your struggles and earn your trust.

Trust problems may also be caused by a lack of self-assurance, a feeling of inadequacy, or a general lack of security.
It could be tough for you to accept that your spouse is dedicated to and interested in you alone.
Many partnerships have doubts and suspicions, and the root of the problem may be fear.
For your spouse to understand you and maybe assist ease some of your anxieties, it is vital to discuss them with them.

Unspoken fears that manifest as doubts and suspicions can be very difficult for your spouse to deal with.

As a result, he or she may grow frustrated and think it's impossible to earn your trust and may even give up trying.
If you don't express your worries and doubts, they might fester inside of you.

When you share your worries, you may realize that you have been worrying excessively more often than not.
Open communication about your emotions and concerns may assist to reduce them, which will increase your ability to trust.

One of the most crucial ways to maintain a strong connection with your spouse during the life of your marriage is to listen to and communicate with them freely and honestly frequently.

How to create and keep trust

There are numerous ways to establish and uphold trust with your spouse.
Being open, honest, and transparent with your spouse about your emotions, thoughts, and actions is one of the most crucial things you can do.
Being consistent, dependable, and dependable is another way to foster trust in your marriage.
Simple acts of support, like running errands for your spouse or being on time, may go a long way toward letting them know you are there for them and that they can depend on you.

Like anything else, trust requires care to flourish.
To stay healthy, it needs ongoing care and attention.
A strong and supportive lifelong commitment depends on both of you realizing that trust is one of your marriage's fundamental components.

How to Rebuild Trust in Your Marriage

Reassembling the Pieces
Reestablishing the feeling of security required for a marriage to prosper and keep expanding requires a lot of time and work.
Many couples who wish to get back on track might get trapped trying to recover from the agony brought on by a breach of trust.

According to research, to successfully move beyond a loss of trust, couples must address the following five issues:

understanding the subtleties
letting go of the rage
displaying dedication
restoring faith
reestablishing the connection

Both of you must reaffirm your commitment to your marriage and one another to restore trust, regardless of who was at fault or who was the betrayer.

Recognize the Details

There are always two sides to every story, even in situations when treachery seems obvious.

The offending partner should be forthright and truthful with facts and provide concise responses to all of their partner's queries.

The party that has been deceived will have a better perspective as a result.
What, when, and where happened?
What emotions or issues might have led to this situation?
Which mitigating factors existed?

Release your rage
Trust violations of any kind may have negative effects on one's mental, emotional, and physical health.
Partners can have eating or sleeping issues.
They might be easily triggered or easily irritated by trivial things.

Betrayed partners must tune in and consider all their feelings, despite the temptation to bury their anger and other negative emotions.
Think about how your partner's betrayal will affect both you and other people.

Consider all the uncertainties that have arisen as a result of how your life has been interrupted.
Tell your lover about all of these emotions.
It is suggested for everyone, including the offending spouse, to vent any resentment and anger they may have been holding in since the occurrence.

Show dedication
Both sides, particularly the one who feels betrayed, may be doubting their

dedication to the marriage and wondering whether it is still the correct choice for them or even if it can be saved.

Acts of empathy, such as sharing suffering, annoyance, and rage; expressing sorrow; creating a safe environment for the acknowledgment and validation of wounded sentiments, may be therapeutic for both parties.

Building on this, specifying what each party expects from the marriage may help the couple realize that going forward with it comes with clear obligations that each party has decided to meet.

To make the marriage work, both sides must collaborate to determine what is needed to maintain commitment.
Avoid using terms that might cause disagreement when expressing this, such as "always," "must," "never," and "should," when characterizing your spouse or what you perceive, expect, or desire from them.
Instead, utilize non-blaming "I" phrases and terms that encourage open communication.
As opposed to "You never put me first," choose "I need to feel like a priority in your life."

Increasing Trust
To get your marriage back on track, you must both agree on clear objectives and time frames.

Recognize that restoring trust involves patience and the following:

Choose whether to forgive or be forgiven.
Try to let go of the past by choosing to love.
Although it could take some time to complete this objective, the important thing is to remain committed.

Be receptive to developing yourself.
With just pledges and declarations of forgiveness, damaged trust cannot be restored.
For the problems to remain dormant, both spouses must recognize, investigate, and work on the root reasons for the betrayal.

Be conscious of your deepest emotions and express your ideas.
Nothing will change if one party is allowed to dwell on the event or deed that caused the trust to be broken.
Instead, it's crucial to address the specifics freely and let all your grief and fury out.

need it to function.
Lip service and further falsehoods have no place in the process.
Be sincere and genuine in your desires.
Once both parties have given serious consideration to the aforementioned issues, discuss your objectives openly and check in often to make sure you are on track.

For the Criminal

It could be difficult or even painful to be reminded of your wrongdoings as the one who harmed the connection.
But keep in mind that the process of repair and recuperation requires the aforementioned stages.
You work on them as you:

If you were the one in your marriage who lied, cheated, or betrayed trust, then demonstrate that the bad conduct is gone by altering your behavior.
That entails that there will be no more deception, lying, or other such activities.
From now on, be open, forthcoming, and transparent.

Be sincere, try to determine the cause of the improper conduct, and then explain it.

I don't know statements don't inspire confidence or assist you in identifying the problem's core.

Accept responsibility for your actions and choices, express regret for any harm you may have caused, and refrain from becoming defensive since this will only serve to escalate the situation.

It is likewise counterproductive to defend your actions by pointing to what your partner is doing or has previously done.

The Betrayed's sake

While much of your progress depends on what your partner can demonstrate, keep in mind that your ability to succeed as much depends on the effort you put in.

Day by day, as you go:

Work on comprehending what went wrong in the marriage and why it did before the betrayal occurred.
While you won't be able to forget what occurred as a result of this, you may be able to find the closure you need.

Once you've decided to give your partner another chance, give encouraging comments and positive feedback to help your partner know what makes you happy or satisfied regularly.
Please be aware that it is equally OK to end the marriage after thinking about or doing the aforementioned measures.
Simply be sincere with yourself and your partner, and don't just go through

the motions because you think that's what a faithful partner should do.

The Couple's

Remember to pay close attention to one another when working alone.

Remind each other that you both deserve truthful responses to your inquiries regarding the betrayal.

Relationship Restoration

Couples must try to approach their marriage as if it is a brand-new one after deciding to repair their trust.

Instead of assuming that their spouse would just know what they want, each party must express what they require.

Even though you are in a fresh relationship with the same individual, you shouldn't restrict your trust.
You won't be able to emotionally reconnect with your lover if you refuse to give them your trust out of fear or rage.
This prevents the proper progression of your marriage.

Instead, put in the effort necessary to reestablish mutual support and create a trust to reconstruct the marriage.
Establish a shared understanding of what a healthy marriage looks like to you both.

Establishing date nights, creating a five-, ten-, or even twenty-year plan with your partner, identifying your love languages, and asking your spouse how you feel your marriage is doing or if it is meeting your expectations are a few examples.

Always keep in mind that partnerships take effort.
Even the closest of relationships need a lot of effort to keep the flame alive and develop together year after year.

Getting Expert Assistance
If you address the five concerns mentioned above and keep in mind the wider picture—that getting through this is only possible if you remain strong and commit to working on it together—you may work on creating a better, happier, and more honest marriage.

You may both move ahead by using a therapist's assistance in processing the what, why, and how of what transpired.

To understand what led to the breakdown of trust, both parties must be willing to seek therapy.
However, in addition to couples treatment, you may desire or need to seek out solo counseling.

Couples may benefit greatly from a variety of therapies that are intended to rebuild trust, communication, and connection.
You could even emerge from such a catastrophe with a stronger marriage via continuing effort and treatment.

Chapter 7

Communication in Marriage – Importance and Tips to Improve

You may respond with "love, commitment, honesty, and other similar things" if someone asks you what the true foundation of a happy marriage is.

But how frequently do we discuss the value of communication in a marriage? Simply because two people live together most of the time does not imply that they have effective communication.

Effective communication between the two is crucial for maintaining a happy marriage and developing a strong bond with your spouse.

Non-verbal communication, which includes actions, is just as important as verbal communication in the process of communication.

In the post that follows, we'll introduce you to the value of communication, some suggestions for improving it, and several other related topics.

Communication in a Marriage: Its Importance

Why is communication crucial for a long-lasting, happy marriage with your better half?

What function does communication serve in a marriage?

Here are some examples that highlight the value of communication in marriage:

1. A lack of communication suggests indifference

You may not be able to comprehend or empathize with your spouse if you are unaware of what is going on in their life or of any potential problems they may be facing.

Therefore, it is crucial to have excellent communication. Otherwise, this might gradually result in a loss of interest in one another's life and strained relationships.

2. Improved comprehension

In addition to having a greater knowledge of one another, couples who often converse, share their lives or interact with one another also develop stronger bonds.

There is less chance for misunderstanding or ambiguity when

you comprehend your partner and the circumstances they may be facing.

3. Greater Martial Contentment
A happy and tranquil relationship is more likely to develop if you and your spouse have established good lines of communication.
Better communication leads to more contentment in a marriage since you talk about everything and there are fewer arguments or disagreements.

4. Increased Integrity, Trust, and Respect
You cannot simply keep demanding everything from a marriage without ever providing anything in return.
Therefore, it helps to develop stronger trust in a relationship if you are honest with your spouse and provide and

receive good comments or disclose other difficulties with total honesty.

5. Improved Relationship

Your partner can understand your sentiments and emotions when you communicate with them.

We comprehend that it is not crucial to put the love and devotion you feel for your spouse into words.

However, one of the finest methods to convey your feelings to your partner and foster a closer bond is by being loud and expressive.

Common Errors Couples Make in Marriage and Solutions

1. A marriage with more "me"

The marriage you enter into is for the two of you.

But sometimes we forget that, and your marriage starts to revolve more around you than it does around your partner.

For instance, you would only arrange a vacation when you can take leave, you would only go to locations you favor, and every year on your anniversary, you want your spouse to treat you special by taking you out to dinner.

All of this demonstrates that you should put your happiness or consent above that of your companion.

How to Conclude

You should also take your partner's interests into account.

When you two communicate more effectively with one another, this will be doable.

Talk to your spouse to learn more about their likes, dislikes, celebration preferences, and other characteristics.

2. Yelling at your spouse

There will inevitably be ups and downs in any marriage.

However, it is not acceptable to yell at or say hurtful things to your spouse if they make a mistake, regardless of how little or serious it is.

It is crucial to realize that everyone errs and that when you yell at or reprimand your partner, you say harsh things.

When there is little to no communication in a marriage, words said in anger might more easily hurt the other person's sentiments or emotions.

How to Conclude

Even if you have a good reason to be furious, resist the urge.

Make cautious to convey your message softly and without inciting hostility or hatred.

The best course of action is to wait until your anger has subsided before bringing it up with your partner.

The goal is to avoid making the same mistake again, not to express disapproval or sadness.

3. Avoid competing or comparing

Couples who are married often compare or compete with one another, which is one of the stupidest errors they can do.

Those with comparable professional backgrounds or positions could exhibit this error more overtly or obviously.

With your spouse, you might boast about your accomplishments or professional successes or disparage them for their failures or setbacks.

It is fine to have healthy competitiveness or a competitive spirit with your spouse, but you should never insult them. Additionally, poor communication in a marriage might make things worse.

How to Conclude

The most important thing to realize is that, despite having different occupations, you and your spouse are still one person or are bound together by love, which makes your marriage more important than anything else.

Encourage your spouse when they struggle, and celebrate when they succeed.

There is no place for comparison or rivalry between two individuals who care for one another.

Various Effective Communication Techniques to Strengthen Your Marriage

You and your partner may communicate in a variety of ways to deepen your relationship.
Here are some methods you may use if you want to learn how to open communication in a marriage or how to communicate in a marriage effectively:

1. Casual Communication
You talk about important subjects as well as other absurd events that occurred throughout the day.

You like chatting about some amusing things about life while laughing together.
Because you share amusing and joyful moments with your partner, this kind of communication helps to strengthen your relationship.

2. Discuss Obstacles
Every marriage experiences lows and highs, so it's critical to discuss and jointly assess the positives and negative aspects of your union.
Such discussions support any significant life changes or decisions as well as the growth of the marriage.

3. Provides life.
Communication

Instead of being prompted by a need or demand like the communications mentioned above, this conversation is proactive.

These communications place a strong emphasis on having thoughtful discussions that cover topics like talking about your fears, desires, dreams, and hopes, among others.

Included in this are meaningful discussions that can result in meaningful relationships.

These are very private talks that reveal details about your spouse's private life.

Tips for Increasing Communication in Your Marriage

We'll now go over some suggestions for improving marital communication, such as some dos and don'ts that you should put into practice:

1. Attempt to Be Specific

Make sure to be specific whenever you want to make a point.

Avoid waffling or droning on about irrelevant or random topics.

Avoid making generalizations by saying things like, "You always say this/do this."

You might hurt your spouse instead of accomplishing your goal if you do this.

2. Show respect

No of the topic of communication between you and your partner, it's crucial to treat it with respect.

You may demonstrate your respect for your spouse by listening carefully to them.

When you take the time to listen, your spouse will reciprocate when you need to speak.

3. Never nag or jeer.
Nobody enjoys being teased or nagged, and your husband is no exception.
Every time you want to make a point, you cannot keep blaming or holding your spouse accountable for his prior transgressions.
Every time you tease your spouse, you not only bring them sorrow and anguish, but it also has an impact on your relationship. Your partner needs to feel desired and appreciated.
Additionally, never bring up family members or friends during disputes.

4. Avoid drawing hasty conclusions

Without speaking with your partner first, avoid making assumptions or making up your narrative.

Without even understanding or giving your spouse the chance to explain why they did not answer the phone, you might become upset that they did not do so.

Discuss your concerns with your spouse so that you can learn the truth about their side of the story.

5. Engage in Continual Conversations

Make sure to set aside some time each day for meaningful conversation with your spouse, regardless of how busy you are or how much work you have to do.

Get silly or goofy and laugh heartily with each other if you are having trouble coming up with conversation topics.

To maintain love in your marriage, it is crucial to communicate with your spouse frequently.

6. No-Fault Games

Even if your spouse offended you because they did something wrong, it is not advisable to start assigning blame.

Your spouse may realize what they'd done was wrong and take the appropriate steps to atone for it.

Even if there are no realizations, it is always preferable to make a point gently and politely rather than laying all the blame on the other person.

7. Avoid relying solely on online chat.

Online chatting is a convenient way to communicate when you are away from home or at work, but it cannot replace real-time phone calls or one-on-one conversations.

Sometimes online modes of communication can lead to misunderstandings and confusion and may strain happy relationships.

8. Don't Be Defensive

If your partner needs to bring out some complaints or issues against you, it is important to listen to them intently without being defensive about it.

It is equally hard for your partner to bring his or her flaws in front of you.

Make sure you listen and take effective measures to solve the issue rather than getting all defensive about the whole issue.

9. Show Tolerance

We all have different preferences, likes or dislikes, and the same goes for two people who are married to each other. If your spouse prefers tennis to watch cricket, for example, show appreciation for and tolerance for their preference instead of criticizing it. Because your partner will also become receptive when you do.

10. Convey positive emotions

The majority of us may discuss our concerns, tensions, anxieties, and other negative emotions more often than we discuss our good emotions, such as love, compassion, humility, etc.

Make sure to have more good conversations, such as complementing one another, expressing your love and concern for one another, and other similar sentiments.

More important than we might imagine is the importance that communication plays in a happy marriage.
It's crucial to have clear lines of communication with your spouse to foster trust and understanding, which will lead to a healthier marriage.

You are not being faithful to your spouse if you profess your love for someone but do not demonstrate it through your words and deeds.
Tell someone you trust them if you do.

Communication should be a priority in a marriage.
Your marriage has a decent chance of being happy and healthy if you can communicate honestly.
As it establishes the proper foundation for the relationship, communication should be valued from the early stages of courting.
According to research, honest communication between the husband and wife is the foundation of every successful, long-lasting marriage.
The issue is that some individuals are just not skilled at it.

principles for marriage communication that works well

All of the elements of a solid marriage—love, trust, honesty, and others—don't mean anything by themselves.

These characteristics come together to form an admirable marriage.

The key is in showing that love, demonstrating your faith, and being sincere.

Your marriage might move from excellent to wondering if you can express how much your wife or husband means to you.

However, communication in a marriage involves more than simply talking.

Let your marital intimacy, love, and healthy connection be guided by the communication rules for married couples.

several ways to communicate in a marriage

While verbal communication with your spouse about your emotions, your day, your history, or your aspirations and anxieties for the future is crucial, it is not the only form of communication.

It's possible to communicate without ever saying a word.
The many marital communication methods listed below might improve your union:

1. Verbal exchanges
Everyone enjoys hearing compliments on how they appear.

Everybody enjoys being told they are loved.
Effective pair communication depends on verbal communication, which is the ability to convey your feelings to your partner via your words.
The other person could never really get how much you love them if you don't express it to them often enough.
Being able to compliment your spouse will help them to feel loved, valued, and aware of your feelings.

Therefore, you won't take verbal marriage communication skills with your partner lightly if you understand the value of communication in marriage.
Such communication is essential for a committed partnership.

You must have the ability to convey your happiness as well as your displeasure in words.
If your partner is doing something that distresses you but you remain mute, your lack of trust will simply let the behavior continue.

a couple enjoys a cup of coffee together
You can't live your life holding all of your resentment inside while your wife or husband is around.
It's important and beneficial for your relationship to express yourself.
Don't put off saying what you need to say until it's too late. Instead, express it sensitively and kindly.

2. nonverbal cues and signals

We cannot minimize nonverbal communication while discussing how crucial it is in a marriage.
Humans communicate far more than we give ourselves credit for with our bodies.

Be conscious of the messages your body language is sending to your spouse.
When having unpleasant talks with your spouse, face them and maintain open body language.
Your spouse will inadvertently detect a lack of vulnerability if you attempt to conduct an important talk while slumped over and walled off.

No crossing of the legs.
No arm-crossing.

Your physical presence should communicate to your partner that you are willing to listen to what they have to say and to work through it.

A closed-off posture is only one of several nonverbal clues that you might use to convey good or negative feelings to your spouse without saying a word. Consider and be more aware of how your body communicates your sentiments.

3. Physical deeds
preparing supper.
visiting the supermarket
and removing the trash.
going to get your pregnant wife some ice cream.
These are all actions that you do to demonstrate to your spouse that you

care about them rather than the things you say.

You may show your spouse how much you care about them by doing simple but considerate deeds.
When discussing the value of communication in relationships, such physical gestures are especially helpful for couples who may not be very good at verbal communication.

With this kind of communication, the adage "actions speak louder than words" is relevant.
Your body language should convey to your partner that you are being truthful and open with them.
Make the necessary modifications based on what your body is telling you

so that your spouse can see that you're being sincere.
The keen eye will pick up on warning signs such as closing oneself off, covering your lips when speaking and displaying unfavorable facial expressions.

pair holding hands
Use your behavior to show your spouse that you are honest, loving, and trustworthy.
You may offer them a massage, a meaningful present, or assistance with a challenging assignment.
Your deeds will speak for themselves without the need for spoken words.

Ten good reasons to communicate in a marriage

A happy marriage is built on open communication.
Instead of how much time you spend talking to each other, the quality of your discussions matters more in marriage.
Here is a list of reasons why communication is crucial in marriage if you're seeking explanations.

1. Prevent and eliminate miscommunications
Husband and wife communication might act as a buffer against marital misunderstandings.
Your partner can comprehend you better when you honestly discuss your thoughts, histories, desires, and beliefs.
Marriage communication gives you the chance to fully comprehend your

spouse's thoughts and motivations, which may help you avoid misunderstandings.
It guarantees that you won't be surprised by their subsequent acts, words, or ideas.

Additionally, talking to your spouse throughout your marriage is the greatest way to sort up any misunderstandings you may have had with them.
You may avoid any misunderstanding from hurting your relationship by communicating clearly and being upfront with one another.

2. Gains esteem
You can appreciate someone if they are upfront and honest about their emotions, opinions, and history.

Your partner's emotional openness will provide you insight into their worldview and motivations.

It could provide you with a good cause to admire their deeds, words, wisdom, and abilities.

Your companion will be able to appreciate your fortitude and perseverance if you decide to relate the difficulties you have faced.

3. Promotes trust

Walls of defense do not foster trust.

In every marriage, trust is crucial because it promotes dependability, candor, and genuine intimacy between two individuals.

According to research, trust is crucial to a successful marriage because it allows good communication between you and your spouse.

Additionally, you will be able to trust your spouse more readily if they are open, honest, and vulnerable with you while speaking.

Get to know each other through communicating effectively orally, non-verbally, or via gestures. Constant communication may help a marriage improve with time.

No reason to continue speculating
Will he like this?
Why did she say it, exactly?
As it will save you from spending your time, energy, and peace of mind attempting to guess what your spouse wants, you may concentrate on enhancing communication in your marriage.
The same applies to your partner, too.

You and your spouse will waste time attempting to infer your partner's preferences, emotions, and pet peeves in the absence of healthy marital communication.
Guesswork might also lead to serious mistakes that may damage your relationship.

You may do the right thing and show your spouse that you appreciate their viewpoint by asking them directly for their input.

4. Time-saving
In a marriage, communicating well is key to coordinating efforts and getting things done.
Although being honest may seem like a lot of work, it is better and takes less

time than fixing errors when you attempt to accomplish things with your partner.

You may speak to your spouse about the things that annoy you and the reasons why they upset you rather than waste time arguing about unimportant issues.

It will take less time, and dealing with it will be less stressful.

6. Recognize yourself

Marriage and communication may seem to be complementary components that improve your relationship with your spouse.

However, this relationship has another aspect to it.

You may better understand how you feel and what is important to you in your marriage by communicating with your spouse.

You may not have had time to consider your feelings towards some topics before being questioned about them.

Consequently, communication may improve your understanding of who you are.

7. Increase marital contentment

Look at the research that shows communication to be a key element in influencing marital happiness if you're thinking "Why is communication crucial in a marriage."

You might feel more connected to your mate and fulfilled in your relationship by communicating with them.

If you communicate honestly, your spouse will become your confidante, which will guarantee that each of you remains interested in the other.

8. Develop together

Couples have the option of becoming closer or further apart throughout time.

Couples should always maintain the channels of communication open to guarantee that they develop together.

Your spouse will be aware of any changes if you start behaving and feeling differently via dialogue.

couple sharing a laugh

If you are both open to each other, you won't be surprised by the adjustments and personality development in either of you.

You may fall in love with your spouse's new sides via open communication.

9. Gain new knowledge

Do you understand your partner's past?

Would you want to learn even more about them?

If so, then remain in touch.

You will be able to learn new things about your spouse via conversations with them.

Regardless of how close you are to your spouse, there will always be tiny things you learn about them and come to understand better.

10. Health advantages

The health of your marriage may be improved through better communication between you and your spouse.

On a personal level, discussing your issues and aspirations with your spouse might also help you feel less stressed.

You may use it to sift through your emotions and stop worrying about the future.

last thoughts

It is impossible to overstate how crucial communication is in a marriage.

Fewer misunderstandings are guaranteed by open lines of communication, which also aid in the marriage's holistic development.

Any successful marriage must have open communication, but you can't depend just on one of the three methods mentioned above.

As time goes on, it will require a thoughtful mix of verbal, nonverbal, and physical communication to express to your spouse how much they mean to you.

Inform your spouse of the qualities you like in them, but also don't be hesitant to speak out if something is making you unhappy.

With time, that verbal exchange of openness and honesty will pay off handsomely as an investment.

Chapter 8

Selflessness

Human nature dictates that you put yourself before other people.
When you're in a relationship, this rule does not entirely hold.
You must change the narrative by putting others before yourself if you want your marriage to succeed and last.

What does love in a relationship include being selfless?

If you've ever wondered what selflessness is, you should know that it's an act of giving without expecting anything in return.

This means that you would put your partner's needs ahead of your own.
Similar to that, it also implies that you would see your spouse as the primary member of your marriage, with you in second place.
You will discover how to be unselfish and joyful through this research study.
The lessons/content of this research, titled Selflessness and Happiness in Everyday Life, are based on an experience sampling approach.

Is it good to be unselfish in a marriage?

There are various justifications for why selflessness is crucial.
The first benefit is that it enables you to defend your lover when they mistreat you.

Long-term conflict is reduced by doing this.
Additionally, being unselfish makes your spouse happy, which will motivate them to do the same for you.

Your view on love will alter when you are in a relationship where you are unselfish because you will be eager to make your spouse happy every day when you wake up.

Putting your spouse first is one of the finest ways to be unselfish in a marriage.
You must think about your partner's needs and goals before your own.
Being unselfish entails believing that your spouse must be content and joyful.

As a result, you will constantly put yourself in your partner's position to understand how they are feeling and how you can support them.

If you're unsure if it's possible to be too unselfish, read this study by Elizabeth Hopper.
This article offers advice on how to respect your partner's demands while still being unselfish toward them.

How to be unselfish in a relationship: 15 easy steps
Being unselfish is one strategy to use if you want to build a lasting connection. Many long-lasting relationships were made possible by the partners' selflessness.

Here are some suggestions on being unselfish in a partnership.

1. Adopt the proper perspective
You must keep in mind that, while you are in a relationship, the world does not revolve around you.
Instead, you have a partner to whom you are devoted.
Therefore, before making any decisions, you should also consider their sentiments and emotions.
It's important to keep in mind that your spouse has needs and desires that must also be met.
You will demonstrate the genuine meaning of selfless love if you constantly have your spouse in mind.

2. Prepare to make concessions

must be willing to compromise and learn how to be more altruistic in a marriage.

For instance, be prepared to accommodate your partner's preferences if you want to go on a date with them but they have a certain location in mind.

Similar to this, don't refuse your partner's desire to watch a certain movie if you want to.

When you do this often, you unintentionally urge your spouse to be as unselfish.

3. Consider the perspective of your spouse.

Another method to practice selflessness in marriage is to consistently attempt to see things from your partner's perspective.

You don't have to disagree with your spouse when they complain.
Instead, make an effort to comprehend them by giving their words some thought.
Likewise, kids should have the entire right to be heard and understood if they have any opinions.
Being unselfish allows your spouse the opportunity to express their thoughts.

4. Demonstrate forgivingness
You may not know how to be unselfish in a relationship if you find it difficult to forgive.
Even though it is very tough and unpleasant, you should always strive to forgive your spouse when they upset you.

You must keep in mind that you could find yourself in their shoes tomorrow and want their pardon.

As a result, practicing selfless love necessitates teaching your spouse to forgive you.

5. Be sincere

One of the things to avoid while learning how to be unselfish in a relationship is expecting nothing in return.

You shouldn't act kindly toward your spouse if you anticipate receiving anything in return.

6. Do not bring up the favors you have performed for them.

Reminding your spouse of your accomplishments can help you avoid gaslighting them and demonstrate your selflessness in marriage.

By doing this, you are implying that since you previously showed them kindness, you want them to treat you with extreme caution.

Do not immediately remind your spouse of your nice actions, even if you believe they are being shown a lack of gratitude.

7. Show them sincere appreciation

One of the rules to follow when it comes to being unselfish in a relationship is to sincerely respect your mate.

Thank your spouse for whatever they do for you, no matter how little.

Make it clear to your spouse that you like being with them and value their efforts to brighten your day.

8. Go above and above for them

Going above and beyond for each other might sometimes be the difference between a happy marriage and one that fails.

Learn to go above and above if you want to know how to be unselfish in a relationship.

Your spouse will be astonished if you do this often, and they will owe you money.

You will grow to love your mate more when you go above and beyond for them.

9. Listen attentively.

Being an excellent listener is one method for demonstrating selflessness in relationships.

It's crucial to do more than simply hear when your spouse is speaking to you; you also need to pay attention.
You'll be able to distinguish between the crucial and minor nuances of the discussion when you listen to your companion.

10. Every day, show compassion.
Pair in park
Putting this hack into practice is one way to be unselfish in a marriage.
Make it a point to do at least one kind thing for your lover every day when you get up.
You must keep in mind that doing this would do much to make them happy.
Additionally, it would inspire them to do the same for you, strengthening your marriage.

11. Complement rather than criticize

Instead of angrily criticizing your spouse when they do anything wrong, find a way to thank them.

Additionally, it is advised to use constructive criticism rather than destructive criticism when you must fix them.

This will enable you to distinguish between the act and the person.

12. Support charities

Selflessness in a marriage may be cultivated via extracurricular pursuits. Giving to charities is one of them.

Helping the less fortunate puts your heart in a position to be compassionate and to love selflessly.

One way we are reminded that everyone deserves love is through giving to charity.

13. Show your spouse some patience.
If you've wondered what it means to be unselfish, read on.
Using patience is one strategy for responding to this.
You must be patient with your spouse if they take a long time to get used to anything.

Being patient with your partner makes you more unselfish since you are more able to comprehend their circumstances.

14. Accept their family and friends as your own.

Being at peace with your partner's friends and family is a need for selflessness in marriage.

This indicates that you see your spouse's family as a part of your own.

Anything you do will thus be repeated for your family and friends.

Most of the time, your spouse would be satisfied with who you are as a person and would want to behave similarly.

15. Consider your partner's shortcomings

Another strategy for being unselfish in a relationship is to accept your spouse as they are.

Every person has flaws.

Ignoring and refraining from passing judgment on others for their flaws requires compassion and selflessness.

Therefore, even if it bothers you, always be prepared to tolerate your spouse's shortcomings.
With this kind deed, you may be sure that they will reciprocate for you.
Check out Jane Greer's book What About Me to learn how to avoid selfishness from wrecking your relationship with your spouse.
This book assists you in developing more selflessness so that you may save your marriage.

The lesson
This article has provided you with the necessary information to get started if you don't know how to be unselfish in a relationship.
One thing to keep in mind is that your marriage has a better chance of

success if you are unselfish toward your spouse.

www.ingramcontent.com/pod-product-compliance
Lightning Source LLC
LaVergne TN
LVHW010554160826
845677LV00013B/3120

9798353163558